Buddy BOOKS
Prehistoric Animals

Giant Ape

ABDO
Publishing Company

A Buddy Book
by
Michael P. Goecke

VISIT US AT
www.abdopub.com

Published by Buddy Books, an imprint of ABDO Publishing Company, 4940 Viking Drive, Edina, Minnesota 55435. Copyright © 2003 by Abdo Consulting Group, Inc. International copyrights reserved in all countries. No part of this book may be reproduced in any form without written permission from the publisher.

Printed in the United States.

Edited by: Christy DeVillier
Contributing Editor: Matt Ray
Graphic Design: Deborah Coldiron
Image Research: Deborah Coldiron
Illustrations: Deborah Coldiron, Denise Esner
Photographs: Digital Stock, Digital Vision, Steve McHugh, Photodisc, Photospin

Library of Congress Cataloging-in-Publication Data

Goecke, Michael P., 1968-
    Giant ape / Michael P. Goecke.
        p. cm. -- (Prehistoric animals. Set I)
    Includes index.
    Contents: Prehistoric animals—Giant ape—What did it look like?—Discovery—Dragon teeth—When did it live and where?—Orangutans and gorillas—How do we know?—How did it disappear?
    ISBN 1-57765-967-8
    1. Gigantopithecus—Juvenile literature. [1. Gigantopithecus. 2. Apes, Fossil. 3. Apes. 4. Prehistoric animals.] I. Title.

GN282.6 .G64 2003
569'.88—dc21

                                                                              2002028197

Table of Contents

Prehistoric Animals

Crocodiles have been around for millions of years. They have been here since the time of dinosaurs. So have horseshoe crabs and cockroaches.

But most animals from the prehistoric world are not alive today. Woolly mammoths, saber-toothed cats, and other prehistoric animals died out long ago. Scientists study fossils to learn about these amazing animals.

Crocodiles lived in the prehistoric world.

Prehistoric Animals

The Giant Ape

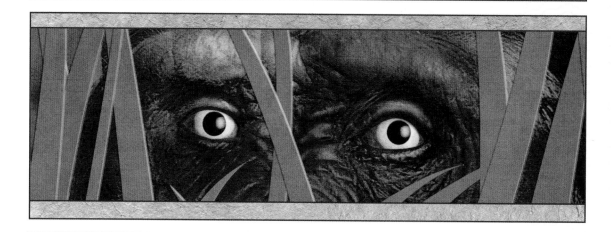

Gigantopithecus blacki
(jy-gan-toh-PITH-uh-cuss bla-kee)

Gigantopithecus blacki was a **prehistoric** ape. Another name for *Gigantopithecus blacki* is giant ape. Scientists believe the giant ape was the biggest ape that ever lived.

Today's great apes are related to the prehistoric giant ape. Gorillas, orangutans, and chimpanzees are all great apes. The giant ape's closest living relative is the orangutan.

Today's orangutans are related to the giant ape.

The giant ape probably looked a lot like today's apes. Today's apes have a hairy coat. But parts of their face, hands, and feet are hairless. Maybe the giant ape was hairy in the same way.

Giant apes were probably hairy like this chimpanzee.

What the giant ape may have looked like.

The Giant Ape's Size

Giant Ape

Gorilla

Adult male giant apes were much bigger than the females. Standing on two legs, a male adult was probably about 10 feet (3 m) tall. It may have weighed as much as 1,200 pounds (544 kg). This is almost twice as big as a gorilla today.

How It Lived

Some apes, such as orangutans, live in trees. Other apes, such as gorillas, live on the ground. Scientists believe the giant ape was too big to live in the trees. It probably lived on the ground.

Giant apes probably lived on the ground like today's gorillas.

11

Gorillas walk on their flat feet and the knuckles of their hands. This is called knuckle-walking. Giant apes may have walked this way, too.

Knuckle-Walking

The giant ape probably walked like today's gorillas.

A bamboo forest.

Like today's gorillas, the giant ape ate plants. Scientists believe it mostly ate bamboo. Bamboo is a kind of grass that grows very tall.

Scientists believe the giant ape also ate fruit. It may have eaten durian or jackfruit.

The Legend Of Yeti

There are **legends** that say a giant ape is around today. Some people believe it lives in Asia's Himalaya Mountains. They call it Yeti.

Some people believe a giant ape lives in North America. They call it Sasquatch or Big Foot.

Scientists say there is no truth in these legends. They have found no proof of Yeti, Sasquatch, or Big Foot. They believe the giant ape died out thousands of years ago.

Scientists say there is no such thing as Yeti.

Scientists have names for important time periods in Earth's history. The giant ape lived during a time period called the Pleistocene. The Pleistocene began about two million years ago.

A Geologic Timeline
248 Million Years Ago – Today

Triassic	Jurassic	Cretaceous	Paleocene	Eocene	Oligocene	Miocene	Pliocene	Pleistocene	Holocene
248 – 213 Million Years Ago	213 – 145 Million Years Ago	145 – 65 Million Years Ago	65 – 56 Million Years Ago	56 – 34 Million Years Ago	34 – 24 Million Years Ago	24 – 5 Million Years Ago	5 – 2 Million Years Ago	2 Million – 11,500 Years Ago	11,500 Years Ago – Today

Age Of Dinosaurs	Age Of Mammals
248 – 65 Million Years Ago	65 Million Years Ago – Today

The giant ape lived between 700,000 and 125,000 years ago.

A Map Of The World

Giant ape fossils have been found in China and Vietnam.

The giant ape lived in Southeast Asia. Prehistoric cats, elephants, and giant pandas lived there, too. So did prehistoric people called *Homo erectus*.

The giant ape ate bamboo in Asia's forests for thousands of years. It died out about 300,000 years ago. Scientists are not sure why this happened. Maybe the giant ape ran out of bamboo to eat.

Today's pandas eat bamboo, too.

There are many kinds of bamboo plants.

Why would the giant ape run out of bamboo? Prehistoric giant pandas also ate bamboo. *Homo erectus* may have used bamboo for tools. Bamboo forests can die out for no known reason. Without bamboo, the giant ape would probably die.

Dragon Teeth

People commonly find fossils in the ground. Yet, the first giant ape fossils were discovered in a drugstore.

Ralph von Koenigswald was a paleontologist. In 1935, he went to a drugstore in China. He noticed some teeth fossils that were uncommonly big. The drugstore called them dragon teeth.

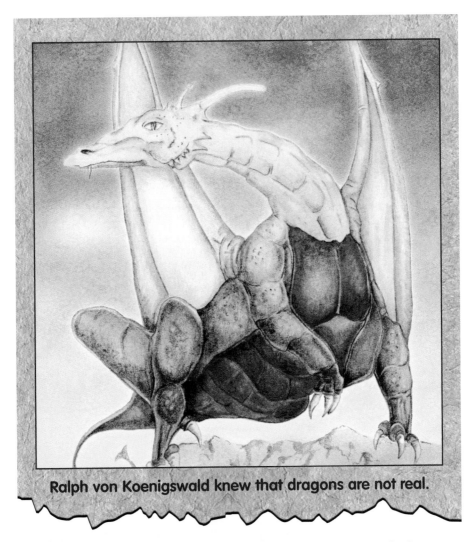

Ralph von Koenigswald knew that dragons are not real.

Von Koenigswald knew the teeth did not come from a dragon. He believed they came from a giant prehistoric ape.

21

Von Koenigswald's discovery led to a hunt for more giant ape fossils. Today, scientists have jawbones and hundreds of teeth from *Gigantopithecus blacki*.

This fossil is a tooth from the giant ape.

Important Words

fossil remains of very old animals and plants commonly found in the ground. A fossil can be a bone, a footprint, or any trace of life.

knuckle-walking to walk using hand-knuckles and feet.

legend an old story that cannot be proven true.

paleontologist a scientist that studies prehistoric plants and animals. Paleontologists often study fossils.

prehistoric describes anything that was around more than 5,500 years ago.

Web Sites

To learn more about the giant ape, visit ABDO Publishing Company on the World Wide Web. Web sites about the giant ape are featured on our Book Links page. These links are routinely monitored and updated to provide the most current information available.

www.abdopub.com

Index

24